THE GREAT DEPRESSION

A HISTORY PERSPECTIVES BOOK

Roberta Baxter

Published in the United States of America
by Cherry Lake Publishing
Ann Arbor, Michigan
www.cherrylakepublishing.com

Consultants: Douglas A. Irwin, Professor, Economics Department,
Dartmouth College; Marla Conn, ReadAbility, Inc.
Editorial direction: Red Line Editorial
Book design: Sleeping Bear Press

Photo Credits: Dorothea Lange/Library of Congress, cover, 1, 30; Harris & Ewing
Collection/Library of Congress, 4, 9, 13; Bettmann/Corbis, 6, 25; Farm Security
Administration/Library of Congress, 10; Russell Lee/Library of Congress, 14; Albert M.
Bender/Library of Congress, 16; J.A. Mitchell/Corbis, 19; Ernest Lindsay/Corbis, 21;
National Photo Company Collection/Library of Congress, 22; Marion Post Wolcott/
Library of Congress, 28

Library of Congress Cataloging-in-Publication Data
Baxter, Roberta, 1952-
  The Great Depression / Roberta Baxter.
    pages cm. -- (Perspectives library)
  Includes bibliographical references and index.
  ISBN 978-1-63137-618-4 (hardcover) -- ISBN 978-1-63137-663-4 (pbk.) -- ISBN
978-1-63137-708-2 (pdf ebook) -- ISBN 978-1-63137-753-2 (hosted ebook)
1. United States--History--1933-1945--Juvenile literature. 2. United States--History--
1919-1933--Juvenile literature. 3. Depressions--1929--United States--Juvenile
literature. I. Title.
E806.B37 2014
973.917--dc23
                            2014004767

Cherry Lake Publishing would like to acknowledge the work of
The Partnership for 21st Century Skills. Please visit *www.p21.org*
for more information.

Printed in the United States of America
Corporate Graphics Inc.
July 2014

TABLE OF CONTENTS

In this book, you will read about three people living through the Great Depression. The hard economic times that hit the United States in the 1930s brought struggles to many. As you'll see, the same event can look different depending on one's point of view.

1

Arthur Maxwell
Government Worker

I work at the Department of Commerce for the United States. I am a junior economist, so I collect and analyze the numbers of employed people, salary amounts, types of jobs, and other information. Other government officials can then see the state of the **economy.**

When I started my job in July 1929, it seemed that the economy was soaring. People had good jobs, the **stock** market was booming, and prices of goods were reasonable. The farmers, especially those out West, faced problems with low prices for their crops. But I believed that would soon level out and the farmers would be in better shape like the rest of the country.

SECOND SOURCE

▶ Find another source on the beginning of the Great **Depression**. Compare it with the information in this chapter.

The events of October to November 1929 startled everyone. The value of company stocks listed on the stock market went way down. People started selling their stocks to get what value was left. Some stocks became worthless. The people who owned those stocks lost all the money they had invested. The newspapers estimated that by the end of 1929, several billion dollars had been lost.

Mostly banks or wealthy people, like business owners, owned stocks. Many stocks dropped

▲ *Crowds gathered in shock outside the New York Stock Exchange during the 1929 crash.*

incredible amounts in value. For example, General Electric Company stock was worth $73 per share in September 1929 and in September 1932 it was worth less than $16 per share. Other stocks dropped in value more than that. Banks also lost money that they had invested in stocks. This forced the banks to stop loaning money. People were not

spending either. They were worried about losing
their jobs. I was sure President Hoover would have
an idea of how to get out of the economic mess
that became the Great Depression.

President Hoover's staff held meetings to
discuss what the federal government should do

THE STOCK MARKET CRASH

People invest their money by buying shares of companies.
These shares are called stock. When investors hear that the
value of a stock is going down, they sell stock before the
price goes lower. Many sales make the stock value go down.
More people sell and the cycle repeats. If too many people
sell, it causes a crash. When the stock market crashed in
1929, thousands of stocks became worthless. People lost
millions of dollars that they had invested.

about the economy. I wasn't at the meetings, but they asked for my employment and salary data. President Hoover believed that people had spent too much on stocks and that the economy would even out. He said that Americans had always stood on their own two feet and they should continue to do so. He argued that government should stay out of business because government was too inefficient and would slow business down.

I agreed with the president that the country would come out of the stock market crash with stronger growth. But I was wrong. The economy got worse, more people were out of work, and the banks were failing. Newspapers blasted President Hoover and his policies. They wanted him to pay **unemployed** people and spend money that our government did not have. Like the president, I didn't believe the government should run up a huge **debt**. We had to keep the government out of debt to benefit everyone. Institutions, such as churches and charities, should help those in need. Neighbors should help neighbors, and families should take care of each other.

In December 1929, President Hoover lowered the taxes people paid on their incomes so that people would have more money to spend. He met with business leaders to persuade them to keep their workers employed and not cut wages. Unfortunately, businesses and people were still not spending, and people were losing jobs. Our numbers showed that almost 15 million people

President Herbert Hoover led the United States through the beginning of the Great Depression. ▶

▲ *Some homeless people built shack communities called Hoovervilles, where they lived during the Great Depression.*

were unemployed at the beginning of the 1930s. Even business leaders who had agreed with the president laid off workers.

Banks closed despite the government's efforts. More than 2,000 banks failed in 1931. People lost their savings. People couldn't pay home loans, rent, or even buy food and clothing. Many became homeless or moved in with relatives to save money.

In December 1931, President Hoover recommended that Congress pass a law to set up the Reconstruction Finance Corporation (RFC). The RFC would use money from the federal government to make loans to banks. The banks could then loan money to businesses and people. However, the banks did not loan out much money, so the RFC was little help to the country.

The economy was getting worse. More people were losing jobs, homes, and businesses, and banks were closing daily. One big drag on the economy was a bill passed in 1930, called the Hawley-Smoot **Tariff** Act. It increased tariffs, money paid by other countries to buy U.S. products. It made the food grown by our farmers more expensive for other

THINK ABOUT IT

▶ Determine the main point of this chapter. Pick out one piece of evidence that supports it.

countries. Other countries stopped buying crops and livestock raised by U.S. farmers. The farmers lost even more money, and many of them had to give up their farms. Then President Hoover decided that the government needed to raise taxes so the federal government could lower its debt. In June 1932, Congress passed an act that raised taxes on businesses and wealthy people. This didn't help either.

The election of 1932 was near, and President Hoover was running against Franklin D. Roosevelt. In campaign speeches, Roosevelt accused Hoover of making the economy worse. I disagreed. Hoover had done many things to help. He started the Boulder Dam project on the Colorado River to provide water for much of the Southwest and create new jobs.

It was later named the Hoover Dam in his honor. He persuaded the Federal Reserve to give out more loans to help businesses and people. He tried to help farmers get loans too.

When the election was over, Roosevelt had won. He began his term in the middle of the Great Depression. President Roosevelt continued some of the actions that Hoover had started. He also had many new ideas. But the country stayed in the Great Depression for seven more years. I believe that some of Roosevelt's policies made the Great Depression last that long. I hope the country will never have to go through anything like that again.

President Roosevelt signed many jobs bills, creating employment opportunities for millions of people. ▶

Tom Mallory
Civilian Conservation Corps

My pa and I lost our jobs in September 1932. The steel mill where we worked in Pittsburgh, Pennsylvania, closed, and all of the men were looking for work. My pa worked up to being a shift foreman, but I worked there only two years. I didn't know what our family would do for food and a place to live. My grandpa used to tell us about the famine in Ireland that his parents survived before he came to the United States. I was afraid we were facing a famine here. People all over this great country faced hard times ahead.

Ma started working as a cleaning lady, but there were no jobs for us men. Pa's savings were running out, and we didn't know how we would pay the rent. Ma's pay only covered our food.

I decided to join the new jobs program that President Roosevelt has started. It is the Civilian **Conservation** Corps (CCC), one of the work programs to provide jobs for men. I read a flyer about it. They wanted men 18 to 24 years old who were unemployed. They paid $30 a month and provided room and board.

I trained for the CCC at Camp Roosevelt in Virginia. The CCC sent $25 a month back to my

THINK ABOUT IT

▶ Determine the main point of this paragraph. Pick out two pieces of evidence that support it.

▲ *Government posters advertised job opportunities through work programs including the CCC.*

folks and I kept $5. My folks would be able to pay for both rent and food. Ma cried when I left, but Pa understood that the CCC was my chance to help. My brothers and sisters were too young to work, so it was up to me.

The CCC was under the charge of the U.S. Army. We slept in **barracks** and wore uniforms, much like army clothes. Our camp leaders woke us up before dawn with a bugle call. We performed exercises, ate at the mess hall, and then were set to work. We built cabins at Camp Roosevelt, but the word was that we would ship out to the West.

I got my assignment at the Lincoln National Forest in New Mexico. We rode through Oklahoma and Texas into New Mexico. I had never seen such awful land. They said that there used to be farms there, but all we could see were piles of dirt. I heard about the Dust Bowl, and now I had seen it. The area had little rain for several years and the land was overused. The soil became very

THE LEGACY OF THE CCC

The CCC had men working in every state in the country. The men planted over a billion trees, built 47,000 bridges and 318,000 temporary dams, and carried out many other projects. From 1933 to 1942, 2.9 million men served in the CCC.

dry and nothing could grow. Dust storms filled the skies, and farmers could not produce food.

I worked on **erosion** control projects in the Lincoln National Forest. We built small dams in gullies to slow the water when it rained. I couldn't imagine rain in this dry country. But one local boy in the CCC said that when it rained, it poured, and the water rushed down the streams. We also planted

▲ *Young men work at a CCC logging camp in Michigan in 1934.*

trees. Some people called us "Roosevelt's Tree Army"
or "soil soldiers." I guess both names fit, as we
planted thousands of trees. Their roots helped keep
the soil in place.

The area is pretty with large pine trees. It's a national forest, and the altitude is pretty high. We worked until lunch, which we brought with us, and then worked through the afternoon until four o'clock. After we cleaned up, there were announcements made at five, and then we ate dinner. After the meal, it was free time. Many men took classes. Some learned to read and write. I took a blacksmithing class, just because it was interesting to me. Some nights we played baseball or read books from the library.

One section of our camp was a group of CCC men who were training to be forest firefighters. It would be exciting to be a firefighter, probably a lot like handling the heat of a steel mill. But I really liked planting trees and learning about building.

ANALYZE THIS

▶ Analyze two of the accounts of the Great Depression. How are they different, and how are they the same?

▲ *CCC workers fight a forest fire in Washington in 1937.*

After my six-month **enrollment** time was up,
I learned I could sign up for another six months.
My pa had found some part-time work, but it was
still not enough to support the family. I enjoyed the
CCC work, so I signed up again. I was doing
something important, and I had money to send to
my folks every month.

Clara Jennings

12-year-old Girl

Father lost his business in 1931, and my family's life changed drastically. He owned a loan company in New York City, but business had been bad since 1929 when the stock market crashed. Father lost all of his savings when the bank closed.

My family had always been wealthy. But our circumstances changed. When the banks closed, my father couldn't get money to loan and had to close his business. Our family had less money to spend. We couldn't keep our cook because Mother couldn't pay her. Mother started cooking, and I was amazed that she knew how. I had never seen her make anything except a cup of tea.

Father told us about the business closing and said that he and my brother Clarence would look for jobs. I sympathized with Clarence because I know he wanted to go to college the next year. There was no longer enough money for college tuition. By January 1934, Father had not found a job. Clarence earned some money by running errands for grocery stores and other businesses.

Mother and I walked to the market one day for a few groceries. On our way home I saw Mr. Benton,

THINK ABOUT IT

▶ Determine the main point of this chapter. Pick out two pieces of evidence that support it.

one of Father's friends. He was standing in a **breadline**. Mother said to not embarrass him by saying anything, so we went on past. After we got home, I heard Mother send Clarence out with a basket of food for the Benton family. While we still had food, she would share it with friends.

Mother planned to sew for people if she could find anyone who would pay her. I didn't even know she could sew. My mother used to spend her time volunteering for the Women's Club and the Garden Club.

Mother found some sewing jobs, and she was busy, so I had more chores. I cleaned and cooked some things. I wished I could cook a real meal with a roast, vegetables, and a pie. Instead, we cooked soup with a few vegetables, a small piece of the cheapest meat, and lots of potatoes. Sometimes we had meatless meatloaf, made with rice, peanuts, and cottage cheese. It was awful, but it filled us up.

▲ *Men waited in long lines for bread and other free items during the Great Depression.*

Because I helped out so much, Mother sometimes gave me a dime to go to the movies. The movies helped me escape from the hard times around me. I saw *It Happened One Night.* That actor Clark Gable is handsome. Most of the time, we couldn't spend money on movies, so we listened to the radio. Clarence loved *The Lone Ranger.* Even Father laughed at George Burns and Gracie Allen on *The Adventures of Gracie.*

In March 1934 we lost our house. Father borrowed money from a bank to buy the house, and we couldn't pay the loan back. The bank said we had to move. Father sold our car. The money helped us start over. Some of my friends had already moved, and now it was our turn. At least we could go live with my grandparents in the country outside New York City.

SECOND SOURCE

▶ Find another source on the Great Depression. Compare the information there with the information in this source.

My grandparents didn't have a farm, but they lived on ten acres of land. Father said we would grow vegetables and raise chickens and survive this Great Depression. I didn't know Father knew anything about growing things. Mother was the only one who grew anything, and that was flowers for the Garden Club.

THE END OF THE GREAT DEPRESSION

The Great Depression lasted from 1929 to the early 1940s. President Roosevelt's policies helped some people find jobs, but the country's economy didn't recover until the start of World War II. Industries began building materials and machines needed for the war. Jobs returned and money began to be available for loans.

▲ *The government encouraged families to can food and store it in cellars to prepare for unexpected hard times.*

By that summer, we were getting by at my grandparents. Father and Grandfather planted a garden. It took a lot of work to plant all the vegetables and keep the weeds out. One of my jobs was to feed the chickens and gather eggs. We learned to preserve our food by canning vegetables. At the end of the summer, our cellar was filled with jams, pickled vegetables, and sauces for the long winter ahead.

I tried to be grateful for what we had. My family was fortunate to have food to eat and a place to live. We survived the Great Depression and became even stronger.

LOOK, LOOK AGAIN

Look at this photograph of a homeless family living out of their car and in a tent during the Great Depression. Answer the following questions:

1. What might a government worker notice about this photograph?

2. What would a CCC worker think about this photograph? What might he tell his friends about it?

3. What would a young girl from a formerly wealthy family feel after seeing this photograph?

GLOSSARY

barracks (BAR-uhks) a building or a group of buildings that soldiers live in

breadline (BRED-line) a line of people waiting to receive free bread or other food

conservation (kahn-sur-VAY-shuhn) the protection or preservation of valuable things

debt (det) an amount of money or something else that is owed

depression (di-PRESH-uhn) a time when businesses do badly and more people become poor

economy (i-KON-uh-mee) the way that a country runs it industries, trade, and finance

enrollment (en-ROHL-ment) the action of putting your name on a list to join up for something

erosion (i-ROH-zhuhn) the gradual wearing away of soil or land by water or wind

stock (STOK) a share of a company that is bought by a person who invests in the company

tariff (TA-riff) a tax charged on goods that are imported from or exported to a country

unemployed (uhn-em-PLOID) to be without a job or work

LEARN MORE

Further Reading

Fremon, David K. *The Great Depression in United States History*. Berkeley Heights, NJ: Enslow Publishers, Inc., 2014.

Frith, Margaret. *Who Was Franklin Roosevelt?* New York: Grosset & Dunlap, 2010.

George, Linda, and Charles George. *The Great Depression*. San Diego: Reference Point Press, 2013.

Web Sites

Library of Congress: Americans React to the Great Depression
http://www.loc.gov/teachers/classroommaterials/presentationsandactivities/
presentations/timeline/depwwii/depress/hoovers.html
Find out about Hoovervilles through photographs on this Web site.

PBS Kids, Learning Adventures in Citizenship: The Great Depression in New York
http://www.pbs.org/wnet/newyork//laic/episode6/topic1/e6_topic1.html
Learn about the Great Depression and its effects on this Web site.

INDEX

ABOUT THE AUTHOR

Roberta Baxter has written about history and science for students of all ages. Her latest history books include *The Bill of Rights*, *The Battle of Gettysburg*, and *The Dropping of the Atomic Bombs*. She enjoys reading about the history of the United States and the people involved.